SIGISMUND

Pope Pius II
Pope of Rome

Translated by: D.P. Curtin

Dalcassian Publishing Company

PHILADELPHIA, PA

SIGISMUND

Copyright @ 2007 Dalcassian Publishing Company

All rights reserved. No part of this publication may be reproduced, distributed, or transmitted in any form or by any means, including photocopying, recording, or other electronic or mechanical methods, without the prior written permission of the publisher, except in the case of brief quotations embodied in critical reviews and certain other non-commercial uses permitted by copyright law. For permission request, write to Dalcassian Publishing Company at dalcassianpublishing at gmail.com

ISBN: 979-8-8692-3992-1 (Paperback)

Library of Congress Control Number:
Author: Curtin, D.P. (1985-)

Printed by Ingram Content Group, 1 Ingram Blvd, La Vergne, Tennessee

First printing edition 2007.

Letter to Sigismund of Aeneas Silvius Piccolomini (Pope Pius II)

To the most illustrious prince of the blood of the Caesars, lord Sigismund of Austria, etc. To the duke, count of Tyrol, to his secondary lord Aeneas Silvius, the poet and royal secretary, he says the greatest greeting.

As soon as I moved into Caesar's court, he entered me with great desire to write something to you.

But I am afraid of the fashion of the modern age, which likes nothing but what is most like itself. Almost all who write today, although they address one person, use the plural number, as if by multiplying the persons they add more honor and appear more reverent. Which custom is widespread in Germany and prevailed for some time among the Italians. After Franciscus Petrarch, abandoning the squalor of his time, took up the ancient eloquence, and it pleased most to imitate him to speak thus, as the most chaste age spoke of the ancients, came from Greece henceforth Manuel Chrysoloras, who was buried at Constantia, a man of many letters, whose elders, born in Rome, Constantine the Great, after the transfer of the Byzantine Empire, which is now called Constantinople, they followed.

Here the Italians, already penitent to their coarse and convoluted speech, yet having no more light than Francis had brought, brought them back to true eloquence, so that today the eloquence of the Italians seems similar to that which flourished in the times of Octavian, if any Leonardo of Aretine, Guarinus of Verona, Pogius of Florence, He would read Aurispa Siculus, Antonius

Vincentinus, and others who now flourish among the Italians, in whom both the eloquent river of Tullian and the milky stream of Titus Livius Patavinus shine. They now address those to whom they write by singular number, because they mention that both the Greeks and the Latins spoke in this way, as they testify in writing in the letters of Socrates and Demosthenes and Cicero and Maecenas to the greatest men.

And not only the Gentiles, but those whom we venerate as holy men, they claim to imitate Jerome, Augustine, Ambrose, Gregory, who, not only men but the divine herself, who rules all things by her nod, the majesty of adoring words, lend, they say, but it seemed to them that they should confound all the ornaments and charms of the leaders of speaking properly, if, as is the case, they had spoken.

I also agree with these, and not writing in my own name, I compel no one else to give you a letter of what I am to do, fearing beyond doubt lest you give more to the custom of your people than to my judgment, and perhaps think that it is not otherwise to be written to kings and princes than they themselves have prescribed, to whom I wish it is to use a plurality: we command, they say, we will, we do, but this, which has its origin in humility, is wrong to lead to boasting. And kings, when they write, though they have dominion, so that whatever pleases them may have the force of law, yet they use that restraint, when they write, that those who decree something do not wish to be seen to have done it alone, but with the counsel of others.

And it is not worthy of you that the inferior princes, writing to their superiors, throw away the plural number as fuel for pride, as they literally manifest in sending Caesar the prince of the empire. for the duke of Milan writes: I beg, I beg, I beg, I commit myself to your majesty. for this also has a different reason than that of discretion, and since the lower powers are derived from the superior, it is not out of the question to put down plurality, when the inferior writes, as if the inferior speaking to you, O superior, says, I cannot use the place of others, because you have entrusted them to me. whom I represent to others, not at all to you, because you represent them and me. but as it is customary for kings and magistrates to offer plurality, let nothing compel you. for that is what he was just stomaching. For whom, therefore, should give plurality to princes, because they themselves use it for the sake of moderation.

This is not to honor, but to depress and despise, as if they were nothing without their subjects. to whom, if we wished to be accorded the reverence which they themselves modestly do, we would honorably flee. Nor, since the

Roman pontiff calls himself the servant of God's servants, we, writing to him, return the same title to him, but instead of the servant, we say the father of the servants, the father.

These were perhaps too long repeated at the beginning, which led me away from the purpose. I hope, however, that it has been done with these, that you will either feel with me, or forgive me the following great authors, who address you singularly. which, if you do not do otherwise, at least your singular kindness and innate humanity will warn you.

Now what is it that I would rather write must be completed. And when I came to this court of your cousin Caesar, many things were said to me of your excellent prowess. One spoke of great kindness, another of wonderful honesty and modesty, another preached that you were wise beyond your age, another affirmed that you were generous and justly loving, another, which is rarely found among the leaders of this age, mentioned that you were very respectful of the Latin language. from which things I accepted to both marvel at and love you at the same time, and like a monster I thought that the young prince shone with so many virtues.

However, I was not immediately credulous, nor did I give credence to every voice; I approached others, I questioned the universe, I found them all speaking with one mouth. and these things were not enough with me; I joined you by your side and entered among the crowns of the nobles as a spy, your manners, while you were still ignorant of me, I was spied upon. I paid attention to his gestures, his speech, his countenance; the thing itself won fame, I could not but believe myself, but I admitted my eyes and ears, witnesses of your virtues, and I became a preacher of them, of which I had previously been an investigator. and do not think that I refer to these things in the manner of an assent. For above all things I exhort you to shun all kinds of flatterers like a terrible plague, so that you hate no people more than those who flatter you, who praise you to your face, who prove everything you do, who deny where you deny, and where you affirm. they affirm. they go, I go with Terentius, says Gnatus, and Juvenal, if he says, he sweats. for this is the worst class of men, which most casts down and brings down princes, to be feared not only in youth but also in old age.

Why, however, I have publicly commended you, I will not be silent. The virtues which I have commended will certainly shine in you, but I did not bring them back, so that you might glory, not that you might flaunt yourself with pride or be puffed up. I write this only, that you may keep as much good as you can, that you may keep and enlarge this treasure, that you may have such a disposition that your virtues may increase with age, and that you may become more virtuous day by day, lest you fall into the vice of some, who were good young and bad old, and as it is in proverb: a good chicken, a bad hen. for I desire that you may become a good man from a good youth. which will be easier for you the better you are nourished. And of course you must first of all give thanks to your parents, the most illustrious prince, who thought that your mind should be cultivated, who kept you under discipline and gave you learned preceptors. for this is a very large property and an inheritance, better than a principality. for wealth and power and the honors of this age are the goods of fortune, fleeting, changeable, transitory, which are carried hither and thither as fortune wills. for she has the mortal race as it were in play, and she depresses this man, and exalts this. nor is it great for him to make a king out of a potter, and again a king out of a potter. Hence Juvenal's verse: if fortune wills, you will become a consul from a rhetorician; if this same thing wills, you will become a consul from a rhetorician.

Alexander the Great, having conquered India, in order to show how much he could, raised a certain garden to the pinnacle of his kingdom. But Diocletian, when he had the dominion of the world, laid aside the purple and the bundles, and attended to the watering of the spring vegetables and the planting of the trees. but the goods of the soul, which are self-control, chastity, fortitude, justice, moderation, understanding, intelligence, and memory, adhere to man by a certain fixed connection, and cannot be taken from us except with life. These are truly our goods, while we enjoy the light among mortals, they render life sweeter, after we pass from this world, they give hope of eternal happiness. Therefore, since nature has granted you these gifts, and the care of a parent has increased them in you, I want you to be admonished to preserve the good that is in you. for which purpose I consider the study of literature in which you are already initiated to be most necessary. but since you already see them as if something had thrown off the yoke, it will not be out of the question if I try to bring you back to them. for it is not, as some think, that princes learn letters for this reason, that knowing Latin they may participate with foreigners. for though this is frugal, yet there is another and more noble reason. for since every rule of good living is contained in the study of literature, therefore new ones are expedient. and it is not enough to have imbibed the principles unless it is advanced even further. yet the princes of our age generally relegate them to philosophers or interpreters of the law, as it is not fitting to live well as princes.

I beseech you, therefore, do not listen to them, since no one can become a famous man or a famous prince unless he has learning combined with natural gifts. all, of course, who were famous in the preceding centuries, were chief scholars of literature. Philip of Macedon rejoiced at the birth of Alexander, because he had a son at the time when Aristotle was flourishing. Nor did Alexander, at the age in which you are now, relegated letters from himself, but went to Asia, taking with him the teachers Aristotle and Callisthenes, and did not cease to listen to philosophy amid the noise and tumult of arms. happy, of course, if he loved the vice of wine. Alcibiades and Themistocles, who are considered illustrious among the Greeks, were interested in philosophy. Epaminundas the Theban, who was regarded as the ruler of Greece, paid no less attention to literature than to arms. I passed to the Romans. What can be written more elegantly, what more eloquently than those commentaries which Julius Caesar composed about himself? for he, when he was waging war in Gaul, spent the day with arms and the night with letters. Augustus, his heir, dictated both a free speech and a poem very well, and his most elegant verses in praise of the Aeneid are still extant. What shall I refer to Fabius, Cornelius, or Cato? What shall I say of Pompey, who was so fond of letters, that, although he was consul himself, he did not fail to visit the sick philosopher Possidonius at Rhodes? Cato, being full of Latin learning, despised Greek literature for a long time, afterwards repenting of the purpose, which the young man despised, the old man desired, and did not hesitate, to imbue his old man with foreign literature and to turn his mouth to Greek voluptuousness. It is true that those who, though they had the principality and ruled over the people, still wanted to serve literature. but they do not know the voice of Plato, which is spoken of by Cicero and Boethius as divine. Of course, the state would be happy if it happened to study their rulers with wisdom, which wisdom is undoubtedly drawn from the sources of philosophy. but perhaps you are talking about a myth, which is written about the ancients, who were carefully recorded both in leisure and in business leisure. but this opinion can be conveyed to you by some living people, who, though they preside over matters publicly, and govern the most arduous offices, yet do not neglect discipline.

Leonellus, the Marquis Extensis, writes so elegantly that you would think there is no difference between his letters and those of Cicero. They are called sisters of the Marquis Salutia. The sons of the Marquis of Mantua also handle arms and worship letters. Alphonsus, King of Aragon, to whom both Sicily is protected, and Italy is ready to obey, which was once called Great Greece, who was defeated so many times and finally won and turned adverse fortune in his favor, is never in the camp without books. Wherever he goes, the library follows him. Whether he stays indoors or in tents, every day he either reads or listens to something.

I will go out into Italy and seek the Britons, who are divided throughout the whole world; there is the duke of Clochester, who ruled the kingdom, which we only call English, for many years. This man was so interested in literature that he obtained teachers from Italy, interpreters of poets and orators. Do you see that even this century admits educated leaders? Among these you too may be accused, if you have studied what you have studied, you have been prosecuted. for I will not call you literate because you pronounce in Latin. for although this is beautiful, it is given to crows and pitchforks. When Octavian returned after the defeat of Antony, the raven, having learned Latin, said, Hail, the august emperor Caesar. Hence the Persian saying: who prepared his parrot, chere and picas, taught us to try our words, and added reason, the master of art and the bountiful belly of genius.

But what do you think when a Hungarian or an Italian or a Frenchman comes and speaks in Latin, while you as a young man understand them, other old people hear as if they were deaf. but it will be more beautiful, and then I will call you literate, when you understand the orators, when you will know the philosophers, when you will pass over the poets on your own. This may seem too great and too difficult for you. it is not so. I do not want you to spend days and nights scrolling through books, but for the time being I will explain one hour of each day, which you will give to the letter.

But I want you to be sure that he is learned, whom you listen to, and prudent, whom you take as a teacher, and that you are not deceived by the vain ambition of titles. for no one is more learned because the name of the teacher is either Paris or Athens. but he is an expert, who, gifted with natural intelligence, has studied with watchful care the masters of the authors of the arts, who, having seen and read many volumes of books, has also committed many to memory, who is imbued not only with divine letters but also with secular ones. I would like one of these to live with you, with whom you would speak for yourself by choice, who would not take the time to teach of his own accord, but of your will, who would read when you wanted, and keep silent when you would not. but it will be yours, however many days you want something. and after you have observed this manner for two years, you will, of course, think that you have gained more from the lesson than if you had acquired some province. I praise indeed that your eddies are full of soldiers. for these are they who defend the country, and it is fitting that the glory of arms should stand out to the prince.

but there will be no learned man with you, neither praise nor proof. for just as you feed soldiers, so you could also feed teachers of doctrine, who would teach you the differences and limits of just and unjust and make you a man perfect in every respect. It is not proper for you to follow those who, in order to reduce the cost, exclude teachers, yet feed the lions, as Juvenal says. already tamed and he subjoins it ironically: it is evident that it is lighter at the expense of the beast, and they take more of the poet's bowels.

Therefore, take for yourself a man of great learning and do not spare your expenses, where a huge benefit will overflow. Are you complaining about the benefits? I will mention a few, so that you do not scorn the usefulness of literature. for after you have reached the years of manhood, this will be an honor and an advantage to you, so that the others will be silent when you speak in counsel, since you alone are wiser than all. no one will be able to deceive you, no one will dare to say that this horse and this is unjust, unless he clearly knows that it is true. If anyone presumes to suggest something dishonest, you will be ready to refute it with reasons. if you wish to deal with the people with whom the agreement is to be spoken, they will literally train you; if you wish either to praise or to reproach someone, both Quintilian and Cicero will teach you; if the war is to be undertaken and the works of arms to be given, Vegetius will show the way, and Livy and Quintus Curtius and Justinus and Lucius Florus and Suetonius and Sallustius Crispus and the wedge of historians, in whom are the great courage of Alexander and the warmth of Hannibal and the wisdom of Fabius and the prudence of Scipio and the discipline of Julius Caesar you will find the military audacity of Sertorius and Marcellus, and the sagacity of Jugurte, and the skills of all who have done warlike things. You will never see as much by experiencing as you will lose by reading. If you want to know how to govern a state, you will have to read the books of politicians, which Aristotle composed and Leonardus Aretinus made the Latins. but you must by no means take the old translation for yourself, because it both spoils the eloquence and troubles the understanding too much. Aristotle's economics and ethics will be useful for governing your family and yourself, as well as on the duties of Cicero and the epistle of Seneca and all his books. Franciscus Barbarus Venetus wrote how a wife should be governed, Plutarch how children should be brought up. how you ought to get along with your friends, and how Cicero pays in his old age. He also wrote the same about the contempt of death and other sufferings in Tusculani. how moral virtues are to be embraced.

If you want to know agriculture, Virgil of the Georgics will remind you; You want to survey the state of the world with the eyes of the mind and look at the lives and manners of different provinces, and what each region does and what each rejects, says Pliny about natural history, says Ptolemy, Solinus, Isidorus of Hispalus; you want to know the stars of the sky and the course of the planets and the causes of hail and rain and lightning, returning to Aristotle, Seneca, Virgil; you want to scrutinize the manners of kings and the disgust of rulers, according to Seneca's reading of the tragedies; You want to understand common people and glorious soldiers and the intrigues of the robbers and the deceptions of the slaves, so that you can avoid them, taking Plautus and Terentius into your hands; Oratius, Juvenal, and Persius are ready to teach how vices are to be fulminated; you want to see the custom of the shepherds with Virgil's Bucolicon; you want to know the stories of nations and the feasts and the miseries of the sad and the letters of lovers and the remedies of love, Naso will educate you in verses. nor will Statius be useless to the Thebaids or to the Achilleids, being filled everywhere with heavy sentences. After this, in order that you may become more perfect, and when you think about religion, you will also develop the books of Jerome, Augustine, Ambrose, Gregory, Lactantius, Cyprian, and Leo about the salvation of the soul. You will always have the sacred scriptures at home and now you will look at the old and now the New Testament. what I am now writing, if any learned man outside Italy were to read it, he would most of all accuse me, because among the authors he read I had not numbered Thomas Aquinas, or Alexander of Ales, or Albert the Great, or Peter of Blesense, and Nicholas of Lira, and Alanus, and this crowd of new ones. but beware that you do not listen to them. for though they are learned, they are not able to teach others. I recommend this to you, because I think it is right and I do not dream of it, but I have the most learned men of all Italy concurring in this opinion. Believe me, there is nothing to be learned that needs to be unlearned but train yourself in those authors who are more proven. and we must always undertake the best to imitate. Therefore, you will follow these, you will listen to these and these laws, which I have named for you, if you want to be considered unique and wonderful in the whole world as a knower and leader of many things. I do not, however, advise you to intervene, so that you avoid the company of men. nor do I want you to be solitary, except when you choose to meditate on something and to advance in mental retirement for a time. Nay, I recommend that you be affable, that you be common to all, that you allow yourself to be seen, that now you address these and now those, that you enter into councils, that you attend sermons, that you present yourself to the people and speak through you. I also know that the frugality that men have learned from literature has been proved by experiment. Nor do I praise these men who devote themselves to literature in such a way as to make other things small, such as Democritus and Diogenes are certain to have been, who lived for themselves. They are worthy of all praise and praise, who both served the cause publicly and did not neglect the study of literature, such as Plato and Aristotle and Demosthenes and Julius and Cicero and Pliny and Maecenas and Augustus. and what they had gleaned from literature, they applied to the administration of the state. You will do the same, if you wish to be the best man and prince: you will give your letters their time and their public affairs. now you will judge, now you will hold counsel, now you will handle arms, now you will see to family affairs, and in all these things you will experience what they are literally worth, and combining the advantage of leisure with the advantage of business, you will make a wonderful hope for all about you, and either in thrones or with a few you will have the wonder of a prince in the whole world . neither the splendor of your form, which is excellent, nor your golden garments, nor the adornment of your hair and the pomp of horses, will honor you so much as the beauty of letters and the fame of virtues, whose face, if it could be seen, as Aristotle says, is more beautiful than Lucifer or Hesperus. but for this, as it seems to me, you are already incensed in your own right. for when your subjects, coming recently from Athesus, begged your majesty royally to send you to govern the province, you said, I am not yet so mature as to be able to govern the country. a worthy voice which proceeds from your mouth, and which is to be praised by all ages. for it is fitting that everyone should think about what they refuse to bear and what their shoulders are capable of, when there is something to be done; for what Bias says: he shows the magistrates a man, we shall most correctly say of the principality, in which he who keeps moderation is more like gods than men. for it is not difficult to maintain self-control in poverty, but as Martial says, it is difficult not to surrender one's character to riches. A great capacity for sin follows the principality, there is the irritation of the throat, an abundance of wine and cheeses of all kinds of food, and the glorious glory of the month, to use the words of Lucan. There are beautiful women who fascinate the minds and eyes of young men with their eyes, with their words, with their kisses, and with their embraces. There are corrupters, sycophants, jokers, players, who are trying to storm the citadel of youth from every side. that worshiper of greed makes marketable justice. take it, says he, and keep it recommended. He who gives is a very liberal man and has much to give. Another provokes anger;

Sempronius has sinned against you, says he, take up the sword and avenge the crime. will you then inflict an injury on a prince, which even a private person would not leave unpunished? A beautiful woman, says another, loves you and dies for your love.

Why do you not sympathize and pity the young man and rejoice with him? let us go hunting, said the robust man. Why are you numb? the herds of deer and boars are closed, I will give you a beautiful spectacle. come, send these old men to protect the state; but those to whom it is the cause of living in the palace, what do you say, prince? The meal is already brought, and they are getting cold, come while it is still hot and before the rabbit stops smoking. the best shrimp and wild boar and mushrooms on the table. Why do you stand and lose so much pleasure? Many recommend vices, few virtues. What will a youth do, whose age is short and vigorous, and whose mind is by nature inclined to lust? Old men can scarcely resist so many flatteries, not to say young men. but some say: the prince will have counsel; the elders will advise what is to be done. First, they will consider the affairs of their country. It is known, but all those who crown a prince seek to make him their friend, and not that they are fit, but that they say what they think is amusing in the council, and every one strives to be dearer; , let the young man be free to follow whom he wills. and because he is inexperienced and has little to think about, he is embraced not by what is expedient but by what he pleases. and certainly, as my opinion holds, a prince must either be mature and trust in his counsel, or so rude that he disposes of nothing in the manner of a trunk, but what the majority advises is ordered to be executed. for he who knows something, yet less than enough, is dangerous to public affairs, and subverts governments by hedges, when he rules not according to reason but according to lust. Hence it is that in the books of kings we find that a boy of eight years old ruled well, whether he was seven years old Joash the son of Ahaziah; for he did not rule, but his satraps administered the kingdom.

But the principality is a kind of irritation of vices, and very few are found who do not go astray when they are freed from everything. from Saul to Zedekiah there were thirty-nine kings in Judah and Israel, among whom only the eight-born are counted, but the rest were ignorant, ignorant, uneducated, impotent, avaricious, proud, hot-tempered, cruel, lustful, slaves to flatterers and folly, who with ambition I do not know what They were born as if to the pestilence of mortals. and yet these reigned among the people of God, and most of these were anointed prophets by the servants of the Lord. and Solomon, although he had obtained knowledge and wisdom from God, could not persevere, but he fell in love with foreign women and was united to them with the most ardent love. and he had wives like a queen of seven hundred and concubines thirty, and the women turned his heart away from following other gods. Nor was David, although he had been chosen by God, shunned vices, for he committed both murder and adultery at the same time, which he had not done while he was a shepherd but provoked it with the permission of the kingdom. What can another do if he has less strength? what youth, what youth? or is there anyone who thinks that the dominion of his years should be entrusted to him, when the stronger fence of age fails under him? indeed you are wise, who trusted your cousin and your blood rather than others, and did not wish to assume dominion before you had acquired skill. another, perhaps, would have done otherwise, who, inflated by the opinion of the bird, would have said, "What is this obedience to me?" I already want to be free, I already know good and bad, what is better than to rule? I will say to him, do it, and he will do it; It's time to fly.

Thus, the son of Daedalus, as it is in the fables. and when the father had prepared a row of wings for himself and his son with wax and pitch, that he might escape the prison of the labyrinth, he asked for liquid air, and, follow me, he said, Icarus, and do not depart from me anywhere. He gave birth so long, as to the fear of art, he remained unknown. but when he had already thought himself a flying squirrel, and no longer believed himself to need a guide, he went forth at his father's command, and began to wander about on his wings, and, running hither and thither, and continually flying higher, he reached a fiery country, where, with the broken framework of his wings, and every feather pierced by the heat of the sun, he fell he did, and fell naked into the sea, which is still called Icarius from his name.

I will continue the stories again. Phaeton, the son of Phoebus, asked his father to grant him what he asked for. His father swore to Stigius that he would deny nothing. the son demanded that the chariot of the sun be entrusted to him. Phoebus regretted that he had gone forth, knowing that he was born powerless to govern so much. but because he had sworn, he could not deny it, although Cicero, in his duties, thought that this oath should rather be rescinded. He mounted the chariot, boasting of Phaetho, and took the reins, and at the same time fancied himself to be both a king and a god; but when he came to the middle of the sky, when the sun could not check the horses, and there they wandered and shattered the whole world with fire, Jupiter was struck by lightning and fell into Heridanus.

By these figures they admonish every poet that, before he dominates and dominates, he must strictly measure his strength, lest he rush under the weight, since it is a burden, not a pleasure, to rule over others, if only we wish to do it with reason and to rule to that end for which kings are appointed. According to the Roman laws, which originated from the Athenians and Spartans, which Ligurus and Solon handed down, they wanted boys to be under their protection until the fourteenth year of their age, after this age they gave guardians to young people at the age of 24. for before this age they considered it a weak age. For this reason, when two Scipios had been killed by the Carthaginians in Spain, and Hannibal was pressing Italy with arms, he was going with an army to Spain, and would avenge his father and uncles. At last, when there was no one else who could claim to advance, the province was obtained by necessity rather than by the will of the senate. The Carthaginians, when their emperor, Hamilcarus, had died, refused to entrust the government to his son, who was still young. Nor was Anibal created leader of the Penos until the year that he had succeeded his father had been killed. Massinissa, king of Numidia, dying, commended his sons, because they were young, to the Roman people, and especially to the family of Cornelius. What do you count the deeds of the Gentiles? The sacred canons forbid anyone to become a presbyter or pontiff before the twenty-fourth year. Let us refer to something from the Old Testament, for even there the plans of the young men for the government of the country seem premature. After the death of Solomon, who reigned over the twelve tribes, his son Rehoboam came to Sichen, where all Israel had gathered to make him king. And the multitude said, thy father hath laid upon us a most severe yoke; therefore, thou now abate a little of thy father's rule and of the most severe yoke, and we will serve thee. who said, go on the third day and return to me. When the people had departed, the king took counsel with the elders, who answered: if you obey these people today and cease their request and speak gentle words to them, they will be your servants forever. but he left the counsel of the old men and used the youths who had been brought up with him, who said to him: thus, shall you speak to this people: my little finger is thicker than my father's back, and now my father has placed a yoke upon you, but I will add upon your yoke. Father Mind fell upon you with scourges, but I will give you up to scorpions. And he did so, and the ten tribes, irritated by the people, withdrew from him, and made Jeroboam, the son of Nabat, their king. Israel was divided forever, because the inexperienced king accepted the counsels of the youth. it would have been better if he had been a child, for then he would have listened to the elders. Ahaziah, the son of Joran, was twenty-two years old when he became ruler in Israel, and he afflicted the Lord's people and did what was evil in the sight of God. Ahaz, the son of Joatham, who was twenty years old when he began to reign in Judah, was no different. There was no one worse than Manasseh among the kings, who assumed the government in the 12th year of his age. like him was his son Amon, who reigned 22.

He began to be a year old and was killed by his servants because of the crimes in which he was involved. What shall I say about Joachim and the two Joachims, father and son, or Zedekiah by name, who, having been captured by the Chaldeans at the loss of Jerusalem, first saw his own children killed before him, and was afterwards deprived of his eyes. All these began to reign under the 3rd and 20th year, and because they were inexperienced, they did evil before God, and disgraced themselves and their people.

The opposite of their folly is your youth, who, although he was endowed with prudence as much as can be at this age, and gave the greatest hope of his wisdom, yet he did not wish to be sent to govern a province until he had acquired the strength of age and experience of affairs. and you knew by your own wisdom that you were not going to rule but to be governed, that you chose to endure under your cousin, our most wise emperor, rather than under others, so that in the meantime, while you are growing older, you may follow the royal majesty in mutual counsels, you may know judgments, you may see difficult things, wise men may you hear and become daily more learned by the experience of things. but with these it is necessary to observe what I have said above, that you may give some time to letters, which may strengthen and illuminate the rest of your virtues, with which, if you were, as I hope you will be, properly imbued, when you come to rule you will not be equal to others, but you will be the mirror of all princes and the neighbors will make you the moderator and arbiter of all their disputes. and just as the queen of Sheba and others from the east flocked to see the wisdom of Solomon, so the whole west and north will worship you, and to the fame of your infinite wisdom they will come to see you. for you will be like Josiah, another son of Ammon, ruling your people rightly and not turning aside to the right or to the left.

Come, then, most excellent prince and most brilliant youth, while you have time, devote yourself to literature, acquire knowledge and study. and let it not be a concern to you, if things are in any way renewed in Athens. for your cousin will reconcile them, and for his exceptional wisdom and goodness will make peace, and you, when the time comes, will send you back to your country increased in dominion and virtues. meanwhile the government is rightly entrusted to him, because the region of Athesus needs favor because of the many neighbors who invade your lands and wait with open mouths, how they can devour your patrimony and fear nothing but the royal name and imperial dignity. and although some may tempt some things in the present, it is better to be controlled by the name of a kingdom than of a duke, who, if you reigned, would scorn your youth, and afflict the earth more bitterly.

But I send this, because you knew for sure what was to be done, and you commended yourself to the king. it is mine to exhort you, that, knowing how great the usefulness and how many fruits of literature, you may devote a few hours to the study of which I think you have already been sufficiently convinced, not by my eloquence, which is none, but by your goodness, which you seem to have an inborn love of science by nature itself. but I am now putting an end to it, because the rumor, shouting, and noise in which I am, does not allow me to say more. For I live among the cries that would break the sleep of Drusus and the calves of the sea. There is only one shelter for the whole chancellery, we are several, eating and drinking together, and the ants are not so crowded in their caves as we are in the alleys. The bees hide distinctly in their cells in the beehives, we huddle together in one room like sheep in a fence, and no one can spit unless he stains the other's clothes, and we keep so much silence between us that you think you can hear the pecks in the woods or cornices or frogs in the marshes.

I am surprised that I could only express it to you. but perhaps this is too much for you, who have already cast-off letters as if they were some kind of yoke, and now you are more called upon by your studies than drawn upon. It is a trouble to me that in writing to you I could not sift through the many annoyances which I hoped to read you. but you will pardon both my place and my genius, which is so dull, that he can scarcely decorate what he writes, not in commotion, but in quiet.

Farewell at last and have me as much as your Caesar permits.

From Gretz, on the ninth of December in the year 1443.

LATIN TEXT

Eneae Silvii Piccolomini Epistula Sigismundo

Illustrissimo principi ex sanguine cesarum sato domino Sigismundo Austrie etc. duci, Tirolisque comiti, domino suo secundario Eneas Silvius poeta regalisque secretarius salutem plurimam dicit.

In cesaris curiam quam primum migravi, magna me cupido incessit, tibi ut aliquid scriberem.

Sed veritus sum moderni seculi morem, cui nichil placet nisi quod est sui simillimum. omnes hodie fere, qui scribunt, quamvis unum alloquantur, numero utuntur plurali, tanquam multiplicando personas plus honoris adjiciant reverentioresque videantur. que consuetudo late in Germania patet et apud Italos aliquandiu viguit. at postquam Franciscus Petrarcha, omisso temporis sui squalore, priscam cepit eloquentiam imitari plerisque sic loqui placuit, ut castior etas locuta est veterum, venit ex Grecia posthec Manuel Chrysoloras, qui Constantie sepultus est, vir plurium litterarum, cujus majores, orti Rome, Constantinum magnum post translationem imperii Bizantium, que nunc Constantinopolis dicitur, secuti fuerunt.

Hic Italos, jam scabrosi et obvoluti sermonis penitentes, non plus tamen habentes luminis, quam Franciscus attulerat, ad veram eloquentiam reduxit, ita ut similis videatur hodie Italorum facundia illi, que Octaviani temporibus viguit, si quis Leonardum Aretinum, Guarinum Veronensem, Poggium Florentinum, Aurispam Siculum, Antonium Vicentinum et alios legeret, qui nunc vigentes apud Italos florent, in quibus et Tuliane fluvius eloquentie et lacteus Titi Livii Patavini rivus elucet. hi nunc eos, ad quos scribunt, singulari compellant numero, quia tam Grecos quam Latinos sic locutos fuisse commemorant, sicut Socratis et Demosthenis ac Ciceronis et Mecenatis epistole ad maximos viros scripte testantur.

Nec gentiles solum, sed eos, quos veneramur sanctos viros, imitari se dicunt, Hieronymum, Augustinum, Ambrosium, Gregorium, qui non solum homines sed ipsam divinam, que omnia nutu suo regit, majestatem adorsi sermonibus, preste (!), inquiunt, da, fac, concede, miserere, largire, qui tamen multo ornatius pluralitate uti novissent quam nos. sed visum est illis recte loquendi ducibus ornatum omnem atque leporem confundi, si, ut modo fit, locuti fuissent.

His ego quoque consentio, nec meo nomine scribens, aliter quempiam compello ad te tamen daturus litteras quid agam subdubito veritus, ne tuorum hominum plus consuetudini tribuas quam meo judicio, et arbitraris forsitan regibus atque principibus non aliter rescribendum esse, quam ipsi prescripserint, quibus mos est uti pluralitate: mandamus, inquiunt, volumus, facimus, sed hoc quod ab humilitate traxit originem, nefas est ad jactantiam ducere. reges nanque cum scribunt, etsi dominatum habeant, ut quicquid eis placet, legis vigorem habeat ea tamen moderatione utuntur, cum scribunt, ut precipientes aliquid non se solos videri velint fecisse, sed cum aliorum consilio.

Nec te mereat, quod principes inferiores, scribentes superioribus, pluralem numerum tanquam superbie fomitem abjiciant, sicut ad cesarem imperii principem misse littere manifestant. scribit enim dux Mediolani: supplico, peto, rogo, me vestre majestati commissum facio. nam et hoc rationem habet aliam quam arbitrere, et quia inferiores potestates a superioribus derivantur, non ab re est pluralitatem deponi, cum inferior scribit, tanquam dicat inferior ad te loquens, o superior, aliorum vice uti non possum, quia tu illos mihi commisisti, quos erga alios represento, erga te minime, quia tu illos et me representas. quod vero regibus ac magistratibus consuetudo sit pluralitatem offerre, nichil te urgeat. nam id est, quod stomachabar modo. quis enim idcirco pluralitatem principibus dedat, quod ipsi ea propter moderationem utantur.

Non honorare hoc est, sed deprimere atque contempnere, tanquam nil ipsi sine subditis queant. quibus, si vellemus reverentiam impartiri, quod ipsi modeste faciunt, nos honorifice fugeremus. nec enim, quia Romanus pontifex servorum dei se servum appellat, idcirco nos sibi scribentes eundem sibi reddimus titulum, sed pro servo servorum patrem dicimus patrum.

Hec fortasse nimium longo sunt repetita principio, que me a proposito remotius abduxerunt. spero tamen his factum esse, ut vel mecum sentias, vel sequenti magnos auctores mihi des veniam, te singulariter alloquenti. quod si alia ratione non facies, tua saltem singularis benignitas et innata te monebit humanitas.

Nunc quid sit, quod maluerim scribere, absolvendum est. nanque eum in hanc patruelis tui cesaris curiam veni, multa mihi de tua prestanti virtute sunt dicta. alius benignitatem precipuam referebat, alius mirificam honestatem atque modestiam, alius prudentem ultra quam etas ferret te predicabat, alius te liberalem et justi amantissimum affirmabat, alius, quod raro inter hujus etatis principes reperitur, te Latini sermonis observantissimum commemorabat. quibus ex rebus et mirari te simul et amare occepi et tanquam monstrum putabam adolescentem principem tot virtutibus elucescere.

Non tamen statim credulus fui nec omni voci prebui fidem; accessi alios, percunctatus sum universos, reperi omnes uno ore loquentes. nec ista apud me satis, adhesi lateri tuo, et inter coronas nobilium tanquam explorator ingressus mores tuos, dum adhuc me ignorares, sum speculatus. attendi gestus, sermonem, vultum, nichil non perlustravi, vidi modestum incessum, Latinum incorruptum notavi. famam res ipsa vicit, non potui mihi non credere, sed oculos meos et aures, tuarum virtutum testes, admisi et earum factus sum predicator, quarum antea fueram inquisitor. nec me ista in assentatoris modum referre censeas. Ante omnia enim tibi suadeo, ut omne genus adulatorum quasi pestem teterrimam fugias, ut nullos homines magis detesteris, quam eos, qui tibi blandiuntur, qui te coram laudant, qui omnia que facis probant, qui ubi negas negant, et ubi affirmas. affirmant. ajunt, ajo apud Terentium inquit Gnato et Juvenalis, si dixerit estuo sudat. nam hoc est genus hominum pessimum, quod principes maxime dejicit et precipitat, timendum non solum adolescentie sed etiam senectuti.

Cur tamen te palam commendaverim, non tacebo. elucent sane in te, quas commendavi, virtutes, sed illas non retuli, ut glorieris, non ut te jactes, superbia vel infleris. solum hec scribo, ut custodias tantum bonum, ut serves et amplifices hunc thesaurum, ut sic te habeas, quod virtutes tue cum etate crescant et fias in dies virtuosior ne in vitium aliquorum incidas, qui boni fuerunt juvenes et pessimi senes, et ut est in proverbio: bonus pullus, mala gallina. ego enim cupio, ut ex bono adolescente fias vir optimus. quod eo tibi facilius erit, quo melius es nutritus. et sane debes ante omnia genitori tuo, clarissimo principi, grates referre, qui tuum animum excolendum putavit, qui te sub disciplina tenuit et preceptores tradidit eruditos. hec enim amplissima est supellex et hereditas quam principatus melior. opes enim et potentatus et hujus honores seculi bona fortune sunt, fluxa, mutabilia, caduca, que ut fortuna vult huc atque illuc feruntur. illa enim mortale genus quasi in ludo habet, et hunc deprimit hominem, hunc exaltat. nec ei magnum est ex figulo regem et rursus ex rege figulum facere. hinc Juvenalis versus: si fortuna volet fies de rhetore consul, si volet hec eadem, fies de consule rhetor.

Magnus Alexander subacta India ut quantum posset ostenderet, ortulanum quendam ad regni fastigium erexit. Diocletianus vero, cum orbis haberet imperium, deposita purpura et fascibus, rigandis ortorum oleribus et plantandis arboribus operam prebuit. at animi bona, que sunt continentia, castitas, fortitudo, justitia, moderatio, intellectus, ingenium, memoria, stabili quodam nexu adherent homini nec aufferri a nobis nisi cum vita possunt. hec vere nostra sunt bona, hec dum luce inter mortales fruimur, vitam prestant suaviorem, postquam migramus ex hoc seculo, spem dant felicitatis eterne. cum ergo has dotes natura tibi concesserit, et parentis cura in te illas auxerit, monitum te esse volo, ut serves bonum, quod est in te. ad quam rem maxime necessarium censeo litterarum studium quo jam initiatus existis. quia tamen jam illas videris quasi aliquid jugum abjecisse, non erit ab re, si te ad eas coner reducere. non enim, ut aliqui arbitrantur, idcirco principes discunt litteras, ut Latinum scientes participare cum alienigenis queant. nam etsi hoc frugi est, alia tamen nobilior ratio est. quoniam enim omnis bene vivendi norma litterarum studio continetur, ideo illas expedit novas. nec sat est imbibisse principia nisi et ultra progresaus fiat. seculi tamen principes nostri plerumque illas ad philosophos relegant aut juris interpretes, tanquam principes non deceat bene vivere.

Oro igitur te, ne his auscultes, quoniam nemo in clarum virum aut famosum principem potest evadere, nisi cum nature dotibus adjunctam habeat doctrinam. omnes sane, qui superioribus seculis claruerunt, principes studiosi litterarum fuerunt. Philippus Macedo Alexandro nato gavisus est, quod eo tempore filium habuisset, quo florebat Aristotiles. nec Alexander hac, qua tu nunc es, etate litteras a se relegavit, sed profectus in Asiam Aristotelem et Calistenem magistros secum duxit, nec audire philosophiam inter armorum strepitus ac tumultus cessavit. felix nimirum, si vitio vinolentie caruisset. Alcibiades et Themistocles, qui apud Grecos illustres habentur, studiosi fuerunt philosophie. Epaminundas Thebanus, qui Grecie princeps est habitus, non minorem litteris quam armis operam tribuit. transeo ad Romanos. quid limatius, quid eloquentius scribi potest quam ea commentaria, que Julius Cesar de se condidit? is enim, cum in Gallia bellum gereret, diem armis, noctem litteris dabat. heres ejus Augustus et orationem solutam et carmen optime dictavit extantque adhuc ejus elegantissimi versus in Eneidos laudem. quid Fabios, Cornelios aut Catones referam? quid de Pompejo dicam, qui tam affectus litteris fuit, ut egrotantem Possidonium philosophum, quamvis consul ipse foret, non omiserit in Rhodo visitare. Cato, cum esset Latina plenus doctrina, litteras Grecas diu contempsit, postea propositi penitens, quod juvenis sprevit, senex concupivit nec dubitavit, senium suum litteris peregrinis imbuere et ad Grecam volubilitatem os contorquere. recte hi quidem, qui etsi principatum haberent dominarenturque populis, servire tamen litteris voluerunt. sed norant illi Platonis vocem, que dicta divinitus cum a Cicerone tum a Boetio refertur. beatas scilicet fore res publicas, si rectores earum studere sapientie contigisset, que sapientia haud dubium ex philosophie fontibus hauritur. tu tamen fortasse fabulosa reris, que de antiquis sunt scripta, qui et in otio negotium et in negotio otium diligenter referuntur curasse. sed hanc opinionem possunt tibi aufferre nonnulli viventes, qui etsi rei publice presint, et munera regant arduissima, disciplinas tamen non negligunt.

Leonellus, marchio Extensis tam eleganter scribit, ut nichil inter ejus et Ciceronis litteras putes distare. sororia de marchione Salutiarum dicuntur. marchionis Mantue filii et arma tractant et litteras colunt. Alfonsus, Aragonum rex, cui et Sicilia paret et illa Italie para obedit, que olim magna Grecia dicebatur, qui totiens victus tandem vicit et adversam fortunam in favorem sui convertit, nunquam in castris est sine libris. quocunque it et bibliotheca sequitur. sive in tectis est sive in tentoriia manet, singulis diebus aut legit aliquid aut audit.

Egredior Italiam et penitus toto divisos orbe Britanos petam; ibi dux est Clocestrie, qui regnum, quod modo Anglicum dicimus, pluribus annis gubernavit. huic tanta litterarum est cura, ut ex Italia magistros asciverit, poetarum et oratorum interpretes. videsne, quia et hoc seculum principes litteratos admittit? inter hos et tu poteris nuerari, si quod cepisti studium, fueris prosecutus. nec enim ideo litteratum te dicam, quod Latine pronunties. nam etsi hoc pulcrum est, corvis tamen et picis datur. victo Antonio cum rediret Octavianus, Latinum corvus edoctus, salve, inquit, auguste cesar imperator. hinc Persianum illud: quis expedivit psitaco suum chere picasque docuit nostra verba conari et addit causam, magister artis ingeniique largitor venter.

Quid tamen tibi videtur, cum venit Hungarus aut Italus aut Gallicus Latineque fatur, cum tu adolescens illos intelligas, alii senes tanquam surdi audiant. pulcrius tamen erit et tunc te litteratum vocitabo, cum oratores intelliges, cum philosophos nosces, cum poetas tuapte percurres. hoc tibi fortasse grande videtur et arduum nimis. haud sic est. nolo te noctes diesque libros volvere sed unam dumtaxat cujusque diei horam exposco, quam litteris prebeas.

Illud autem cure tibi esse volo, ut doctus sit, quem audias, et prudens, quem sumas magistrum, nec te vana titulorum ambitio fallat. non enim propterea doctior est aliquis, quod magisterii nomen aut Parisius est aut Athenis sortitus. ille autem peritus est, qui naturali preditus ingenio vigili cura perscrutatus est magistros artium auctores, qui cum multa viderit atque legerit librorum volumina, tum memorie plurima commendaverit, qui non solum divinis litteris sed etiam secularibus sit imbutus. ex his unum apud te vellem degere, quocum pro tuo loquereris arbitrio, qui tempus docendi non ex se sumeret, sed tua ex voluntate, qui cum velis legat, cum nolis taceat. sed tuum erit, quot diebus velle aliquid. nanque postquam biennio hunc modum servaveris, nimirum plus te lucri ex lectione corrasisse putabis, quam si provinciam aliquam vis adeptus. ego quidem laudo edes tuas militibus plenas esse. hi enim sunt, qui tutantur patriam et decorum est armorum gloria principem eminere. sed nullum apud te fore virum doctum nec laudo nec probo. sicut enim milites pascis ita et doctrinarum institutores nutrire posses, qui te justi et injusti differentias et limites edocerent virumque redderent ex omni parte perfectum. non decet te illos sequi, qui, ut sumptus minuant, doctores excludunt, leones tamen pascunt, sicut est illud Juvenalis: e non habet infelix Numitor, quod mittat amico, Quintille quod donet, habet, nec defuit illi, unde emeret multa pascendum carne leonem jam domitum. et ironice subjungit: constat leviore belua sumptu nimirum et capiunt plus intestina poete.

Sume igitur tibi grandis doctrine virum nec parcas expensis, ubi ingens redundat emolimentum. queris fortasse quod emolimentum? edicam paucis, ne litterarum utilitatem contempnas. postquam enim viriles attigeris annos, hoc tibi honoris et commodi erit, ut te in consilio loquente ceteri sileant, cum tu unus plus omnibus sapias. nemo te decipere poterit, nemo dicere audebit hoc equum et hoc iniquum, nisi verum id esse manifeste cognoverit. si quis presumpserit inhonesti aliquid suadere, presto eris rationibus confutare. si affari volueris populum, quo pacto loquendum sit, littere te instituent; si aut laudare aliquem aut vituperare volueris, et Quintilianus et Cicero te docebit; si bellum suscipiendum erit et armis opera danda, Vegetius modum ostendet et Livius et Quintus Curtius et Justinus et Lucius Florus et Suetonius et Salustius Crispus et historicorum cuneus, in quibus et Alexandri magni fortitudinem et Anibalis caliditatem et Fabii versutias et Scipionis prudentiam et Julii Cesaris disciplinam militarem et Sertorii ac Marcelli audaciam et Jugurte sagacitatem et omnium, qui res bellicaas gesserunt, artes invenies. nunquam tam multa expereundo videbis quam multa legendo perdisces. si quomodo rem publicam gubernes scire volueris, legendi erunt tibi politicorum libri, quos Aristotiles composuit et Leonardus Aretinus Latinos fecit. veterem autem translationem tibi nequaquam assumes, quia et eloquentiam vitiat et intellectum nimis vexat. ad regendam familiam et teipsum utilis erit economica ethicaque Aristotelis, tum de officiis Cicero et epistole Senece omnesque libri ipsius. quomodo regenda sit uxor scripsit Franciscus Barbarus Venetus, quomodo liberi educandi Plutarchus. quomodo te cum amicis habere debeas et quomodo in senectute Arpinas Cicero. idem quoque de mortis contemptu aliarumque passionum scripsit in Tusculanis. morales virtutes quomodo amplectende sint, et hi, quos modo retuli, auctores et post eos Macrobius facunde tradiderunt.

Vis agriculturam cognoscere, Virgilius Georgicorum te admonebit; vis orbis situm mentis oculis perlustrare et diversarum provinciarum vitas ac mores intueri, et quid queque regio ferat et quid queque recuset, assit Plinius de naturali historia, assit Ptolomeus, Solinus, Isidorus Hispalensis; vis celi sidera et planetarum cursus et grandinis et pluviarum et fulminis causas scire, ad Aristotelem redito, Senecam, Vergilium; vis regum mores et fastidia principantium perscrutari, secundum Senecam in tragediis legito; vis plebeos homines et milites gloriosos et lenonum insidias et servorum deceptiones, ut evitare illas possis, intelligere, Plautum tibi et Terentium assumito; vis quomodo fulminanda sint vitia edoceri, Oratius, Juvenalis et Persius in promptu sint; vis pastorum consuetudinem cernere Bucolicon Virgilianum habeto; vis fabulas gentium et fastos et tristium miserias et amantium epistolas et amoris remedia nosse, Naso te versibus erudiet. nec Statius Thebaidos vel Achileidos inutilis erit, sententiis gravibus ubique refertus. post hec vero, ut fias perfectior, et cum de religione cogites, tum de salute anime Jeronimi libros evolves, Augustini, Ambrosii, Gregorii, Lactantii, Cypriani, Leonis. scripturam sacram semper domi habebis et nunc vetus nunc novum intueberis testamentum. hec que nunc scribo, si quis extra Italiam doctus legeret, me maxime argueret, quod inter auctores legendos non numeraverim Thoman Aquinatem aut Alexandrum de Ales vel magnum Albertum vel Petrum Blesensem et Nicolaum de Lira et Alanum et hanc novorum turbam. sed tu cave, ne istos audias. nam etsi docti sunt docere tamen alios nequeunt. ego tibi id suadeo, quod per me rectum puto nec sompnio, sed viros totius Italie peritissimos in hanc sententiam habeo concurrentes. crede mihi, nichil discendum est, quod dediscere oporteat, sed illis in auctoribus te exerce, qui sunt probatiores. suscipere nanque semper optima debemus ad imitandum. tu ergo hos sequeris, hos audies hosque leges, quos tibi prenominavi, si vis et multarum rerum scius et princeps toto in orbe singularis et mirandus haberi. interveniendum tamen non suadeo, ut conjunctus hominum fugias. nec te solitarium esse volo, nisi cum meditari aliquid volueris et in secessum mentis progredi ad aliquod tempus. imo suadeo, ut sis affabilis, ut communis omnibus, ut te videndum prebeas, ut nunc hos nunc illos alloquaris, ut consilia ingrediaris, ut conciones adeas, ut populo te exhibeas et per te loquaris. scio nanque frugi esse, que homines litteris didicerint, experimento comprobari. nec ego hos homines laudo, qui sic se litteris dedunt, ut res ceteras parvi faciant, qualem fuisse Democritu Diogenemque constat, qui sibi dumtaxat vixerunt. illi sunt omni laude et preconio digni, qui et rei publice servierunt et litterarum studia non omiserunt, ut et Platonem et Aristotelem et Demosthenem et Julium et Ciceronem et Plinium et Mecenatem et Augustum. hi nanque, quod ex litteris hauserant, in administranda re publica exercebant. idem et tu facies, si vir et princeps optimus esse volueris: litteris suum tempus et suum rei publice dabis. nunc judicium facies, nunc tenebis consilium, nunc arma tractabis, nunc rem familiarem conspicies et in his omnibus, quid littere valeant, experieris et otii utilitatem cum negotii commodo conjungens miram omnibus de te spem facies et vel soliis vel cum paucis orbe toto mirandus habeberis princeps. nec tam splendor forme tue, qui est egregius, nec vestes auree aut ornatus crinium et equorum pompa tantum te honestabit quantum ipsarum decor litterarum et virtutum fama, quarum facies, si videri posset, ut Aristoteles inquit, pulcrior est quam Lucifer aut Hesperus. ad hec autem sicuti mihi videtur, jam tuapte incensus es. cum enim subditi tui nuper ex Athesi venientes majestati regie supplicaverunt, ut te ad regendam provinciam mitteret, non sum, dixti, adhuc adeo maturus, ut gubernare patriam possim. digna vox, que tuo progreditur ex ore et quam omnis laudatura sit etas. convenit enim, quid ferre recusent et quid valeant humeri, quemlibet meditari, cum aliquid est gerendum, quia cui lecta potenter erit res hic demum recte se habebit. nam quod Bias ait: magistratus virum ostendit, nos rectissime de principatu dicemus, in quo, qui moderationem servat, diis est quam hominibus similior. nec enim arduum est in paupertate servare continentiam, sed ut Martialis ait, difficile est opibus non tradere mores. magna peccandi facultas sequitur principatum, adest irritamen gule, copia vini et quesitorum undique ciborum et laute gloria mense ut verbis utamur Lucani. sunt mulieres formose, que tum oculis, tum verbis, tum osculis, tum amplexibus adolescentulorum mentes et oculos fascinant. assunt corruptores, adulatores, joculatores, histriones, qui arcem adolescentie undique nituntur expugnare. ille avaritie cultor venalem justitiam facit. suscipe, inquit, hoc et commendatum habe. qui dat perliberalis est homoet habet multum, quod det. alius ad iram provocat; in te, inquit, peccavit Sempronius, suscipe gladium, vindica scelus. tune princeps injuriam feres, quam nec privatus impunitam relinqueret? mulier, alius inquit, formosa te amat et amore tuo moritur.

Cur non compateris et misereris adolescentule et gaudes cum ea? eamus venatum, ait vir robustus. quid torpes? cervorum greges et aprorum clausi sunt, spectaculum tibi pulcrum prebebo. veni, mitte hos senes res publicas tueri, tu letus esto, dum tempus fert. at hi, quibus in palato vivendi est causa, quid stas inquiunt, princeps? jam epule allate sunt et frigescunt, veni dum accipenser calidus est et antequam fumare lepus desinat. squilla est optima et aper et boletus in mensa. quid stas et voluptatis tantum amittis? multi vitia suadent, pauci virtutes. quid faciet adolescens, cujus etas parumper ac roboris habet, et cujus animus a natura proclivis est in libidinem? vix grandevi homines resistere tot blanditiis poterunt, ne dicam adoledcentes. sed ajunt aliqui: consilium habebit princeps, majores natu astabunt, quid sit agendum. primo res patrie censebunt. scitum est, sed omnes, qui principem coronant, facere illum sibi amicum student, et non que sunt apta, sed que jocunda putant in consilio dicunt et nititur perac quisque ut carior sit, nec est, qui libera proferat animi verba et quamvis pura bene consulet, liberum eat adolescenti, quos vult sequi. et quia inexpertus est parumque pensi habet, non quod expedit sed quod libet plerunque amplectitur. et quippe quemadmodum mea fert opinio, aut maturum esse principem oportet et suo consilio fretum, aut adeo rudem, ut in modum trunchi nichil per ac disponat, sed quod major pars suadet executioni mandetur. nam qui aliquid scit, minus tamen quam satis est, periculosus est rei publice et imperia sepe subvertit, cum non ad rationem sed ad libidinem regat. hinc est, quod in libris regum puellum octo annorum bene rexisse reperimus, sive is septem annorum fuit Ioas filius Ochoczie; non enim is rexit, sed ejus satrape regnum administrarunt.

Est autem principatus irritamentum quoddam vitiorum et admodum pauci reperiuntur, qui non aberrent, cum frenis omnibus sunt soluti. a Saul usque ad Sedechiam novem et triginta reges in Juda et Israhel fuerunt, inter quos solum octoboni connumerantur, reliqui vero ignari, imperiti, indocti, impotentes, avari, superbi, iracundi, crudeles, libidinosi, adulatorum et stultitie servi, qui ambitione nescio qua efferata tanquam ad pestem mortalium nati idolia servientes bellis semper indulserunt, pacis atque otii hostes fuerunt. et hi tamen in populo dei regnabant, et horum plerique per servos domini prophetas fuerunt uncti. nec Salomon, quamvis scientiam et sapientiam a deo fuisset assecutus, perseverare potuit, sed adamavit mulieres alienigenas et his copulatus est ardentissimo amore. fueruntque ei uxores quasi regine septingente et concubine trecente et averterunt mulieres cor ejus, ut sequeretur deos alienos. nec David, quamvis esset electus a deo, vitiis caruit, siquidem et homicidium simul et adulterium perpetravit, quod non fecisset, dum pastor erat, sed cum licentia regni provocavit. quid alius faciat, cui minus sit roboris? quid juvenis, quid adolescens? an est aliquis, qui annis teneris dominium censeat committendum, cum sepe robustior etas sub illo deficiat? prudenter tu quidem, qui patrueli et sanguini tuo potius quam aliis credidisti nec dominatum prius suscipere quam peritiam voluisti. alius fortasse aliter fecisset, qui, opinione inflatus aui, quid ad me, dixisset, obedientia ista? ego jam liber esse volo, jam scio bonum et malum, quid melius est quam imperare? dicam illi, fac, et faciet; jam ut evolem tempus est.

Sic Dedali filius, ut est in fabulis. nanque cum pater alarum remigium sibi et filio cera et pice coaptasset, ut laberinti carcerem fugeret, liquidum petiit aerem et, sequere me, inquit, Icare, nec a me quoquam recedas. paruit ille tam diu, quoad timor artis mansit ignote. ubi vero jam se volandi scium putavit, nec se amplius rectore credidit indigere, jussum patris egressus percussis amplius alis vagari cepit, et modo huc modo illuc discurrens ac continuo altius evolans, regionem igniferam attigit, ubi dissolutis alarum compagibus et omni penna solis ardore peruata ruinam fecit et nudus in mari cecidit, quod adhuc ex ejus nomine vocatur Icarium.

Prosequar iterum fabulas. Phaeton, filius Phebi, patrem rogavit, sibi ut, quam peteret, rem concederet. juravit per Stigem pater nichil se negaturum. filius currum solis sibi regendum committi postulavit. penituit Phebum proissi, scientem tanti regiminis impotentem natum. sed quia jurarat, negare non potuit, quamvis Cicero in officiis hoc juramentum potius rescindendum putasset. ascendit currum Phaetom gloriabundusque lora recepit, tumque et se regem et deo similem arbitratus est: ubi vero ad medium celi est ventum, cum solis equos inhibere non posset illique vagarentur et mundum omnem ignibus confragrarent, Jovis fulmine ictus est et in Heridanum precipitatus.

Hisce figmentis admonent quemlibet poete, ut, antequam presit et dominetur, vires suas rigide metiatur, ne sub pondere ruat, quoniam onus est non voluptas aliis imperare, si modo id volumus cum ratione efficere et in eum finem regere, propter quem reges sunt instituti. leges Romane, que ab Atheniensibus et Spartanis, quas tradiderunt Ligurgus et Solon, sunt orte, pueros usque in annum quartum decimum sub tutela esse voluerunt, post hanc etatem ad annum 24. curatores adolescentibus dabant. nam ante hoc evum infirmam censebant etatem. eam ob causam, cum duo Scipiones a Carthaginiensibus in Hispania fuissent occisi et Anibal Italiam armis premeret, iturum se cum exercitu in Hispaniam, patrem et patruum ulturum, Scipio Africanus major repromittens diu per senatum rejectus est, quod quartum et vigesimum dumtaxat annum esset natus. tandem cum esset alius nemo, qui se diceret provecturum, provinciam necessitate magis quam voluntate senatus obtinuit. Carthaginenses, eorum imperatore defuncto Amilcare, imperium filio, qui juvenis erat, committere recusarunt. nec Anibal prius dux Penorum creatus est, quam anno esset occisus, qui patri successerat. rex Numidie Massinissa filios suos moriens, quia juvenes erant, Romano populo et presertim Cornelie familie commendavit. quid tibi gentilium gesta connumero? prohibent sacri canones ante vigesimum quartum annum fieri quemquam presbiterum aut pontificem ante trigesimum. referamus aliquid ex veteri testamento, nam et ibi quoque consilia juvenum ad regimen patrie immatura videntur. mortuo Salomone, qui super duodecim tribus regnabat, venit filius ejus Roboan in Sichen, ubi congregatus erat omnis Israhel ad constituendum eum regem. et dixit multitudo, pater tuus durissimum jugum imposuit nobis, tu itaque nunc minue paululum de imperio patris tui et de jugo durissimo et serviemus tibi. qui ait, ite ad tertium diem t revertimini ad me. cumque abiisset populus, iniit consilium rex cum senioribus, qui responderunt: si obedieris hodie populo huic et petitioni eorum cesseris locutusque fueris ad eos verba lenia, erunt tibi servi cunctis diebus. at ille reliquit consilium senum et adhibuit adolescentes, qui nutriti fuerunt cum eo, qui dixerunt ei: sic loqueris populo huic: minimus digitus meus grossior est dorso patris mei et nunc pater meus posuit super vos jugum, ego autem addam super jugum vestrum; pater mens cecidit vos flagellis, ego autem cedam vos scorpionibus. fecitque sic et irritato populo recesserunt ab eo decem tribus, qui constituerunt sibi regem Jeroboham, filium Nabath. scissus est Israhel in perpetuum, quia inexpertus rex consilia juvenum recepit. melius fuerat illum infantem fuisse, nam tunc senibus auscultatum fuisset. Ochozias, filius Joran, duos et viginti natus annos regimen accepit in Israhel et afflixit populum domini et fecit, quod malum erat coram deo. nec aliter se habuit Achas, filius Joatan, qui viginti annorum erat cum regnare cepit in Juda. nemo pejor quam Manases inter reges fuit, qui 12. etatis anno suscepit imperium. similis ei filius Amon fuit, qui regnum 22.

Etatis anno inchoavit et a servis suis propter scelera, quibus implicitus erat, occisus fuit. quid Joacham referam et duos Joachim, patrem et filium, aut Sedechiam nominem, qui perdita Jerosolima captus a Chaldeis prius ante se natos suos occidi vidit, postea privatus est oculis. hi omnes infra 3. et 20. annum regnare ceperunt et quoniam inexperti erant, malum coram deo gerentes, et se et suos populos pessundarunt.

Quorum stultitie contraria est adolescentia tua, que licet quantum in hac etate potest esse prudentie sortita sit spemque maximam de sua sapientia prebeat, non tamen prius ad regendam provinciam mitti voluit, quam et robur etatis et rerum assequeretur experientiam. sciebas nanque tuapte ingenio, quoniam non recturus sed regendus ires, quod sub patruele tuo, cesare nostro sapientissimo, potius quam sub aliis tolerare voluisti, ut interim, dum etas crescit, regiam majestatem secutus intersis consiliis, judicia noscas, res arduas videas, viros sapientes audias dietimque fias rerum experientia doctior. at cum his servandum est, quod supra dixi, ut temporis aliquod spatium concedas litteris, que reliquas virtutes tuas condiant et illustrent, quibus si fueris, ut te spero futurum, rite imbutus, cum ad regendm venies non par aliis, sed omnium principum eris speculum teque vicini omnes suarum litium moderatorem et arbitrum facient. et quemadmodum ad visendam sapientiam Salomonis regina Saba et alii orientales concurrerunt, sic te totus occidens venerabitur et septentrio et ad famam tue prudentie infiniti visuri te venient. eris enim quasi Josias, alius filius Amon, populum tuum recte gubernans nec ad dexteram neque ad sinistram declinans.

Age igitur, princeps optime et adolescens clarissime, dum tempus habes, incumbes litteris, edisce scientiam et studio te prebe. nec sit tibi cure, si res alique in Athesi sunt innovate. illas enim patruelis tuus componet et pro sua eximia tum sapientia tum bonitate pacabit, teque, cum tempus aderit, et dominio et virtutibus auctum remittet in patriam. interea regimen recte illi commisaum est, quia indiget Athesis regio favore propter finitimos plures, qui tuis inhiant terris et apertis faucibus expectant, quomodo tuum possint patrimonium devorare nec aliud verentur quam nomen regium imperialemque dignitatem. et licet nonnulli aliqua in presentiarum temptent, melius tamen regio quam ducali nomine compescentur, qui, si tu regeres, adolescentiam contempnentes tuam, acerbius affligerent terram.

Sed mitto hec, quia tute scisti, quid esset agendum, et te regi commendasti. meum est, te hortari, ut litterarum quanta sit utilitas quantusque fructus noscens, nonnichil horarum studio tribuas, quod jam satis tibi arbitror persuasum non eloquentia mea, que nulla est, sed bonitate tua, qui ab ipsa natura innatum habere videris amorem scientie. sed facio jam finem, quia rumor, vociferatio et strepitus, in quo sum, non fert, ut plura dicam. vivo enim inter clamores, qui rumperent sompnum Druso vitulisque marinis. unicum est toti cancellarie receptaculum, complures sumus unis in edibus commessantes et conbibentes nec formice tam presse in suis antris quam nos in auleola degimus. apes distincte cellulis in alvearibus delitescunt, nos uno in conclavi velut oves in septis alter alterum premimus, nec spuere quisquam potest, nisi alterius commaculet vestem tantumque inter nos servamus silentium, ut picas in nemoribus vel cornices aut in paludibus ranas audire te censeas.

Miror mei, qui tantum exprimere tibi potuerim. sed hoc forsitan nimis est tibi, qui jam litteras quasi jugum aliquod abjecisti et nunc magis vocandus es a studia quam trahendus. illud mihi molestum est, quod ad te scribens inter vexationes plurimas perpolire non potui, quod te legere speravi. at tu veniam dabis et loco et ingeniolo meo, quod tam hebes est, ut nedum in tumultu sed vix in quiete ornare queat, quod scribit.

Vale jam tandem et me quantum cesar permittit tuum habeto. ex Gretz, nonis decembris anno 1443.

The Scriptorium Project is the work of a small group of lay people of various apostolic churches who are interested in the preservation, transmission, and translation of the works of the early and medieval church. Our efforts are to make the works of the church fathers accessible to anyone who might have an interest in Christian antiquities and the theological, philosophical, and moral writings that have become the bedrock of Western Civilization.

To-date, our releases have pulled from the Greek, Syriac, Georgian, Latin, Celtic, Ethiopian, and Coptic traditions of Christianity, and have been pulled from sundry local traditions and languages.

www.ingramcontent.com/pod-product-compliance
Lightning Source LLC
LaVergne TN
LVHW061605070526
838199LV00077B/7182